Computer Programming
1,2,3!

Computer Programming 1,2,3!

FOR CHILDREN AND ADULTS

By Dwight and Patricia Harris

Illustrated by John Nez
Cover Illustration by Richard Walz

Publishers • GROSSET & DUNLAP • New York

To Victor Goings,
who encouraged the efforts
that led to this book being written

The authors thank Apple Computer, Inc.,
Intel Corporation, and Radio Shack for
their materials and assistance.

ISBN: 0-448-18961-5.
Library of Congress Catalog Card Number: 83-47679.
Text copyright © 1983 by Dwight and Patricia Harris.
Illustrations copyright © 1983 by John Nez.
All rights reserved. Printed in the United States of America.
Published simultaneously in Canada.

Contents

Computer Programming
1,2,3!

Chapter 1

Computers Today

So you have a computer! Bet you play video games on it. But before you get tired of those games, you can learn how to create your own. You can learn more about your computer and what it is capable of doing. The first step is to learn how to write computer programs. And this book can help you. It shows you step-by-step how to write programs so that you can make your computer work for you.

Computers have been around for a number of years. The first computers were large, bulky pieces of equipment that did little more than simple arithmetic. The concept of the computer was first formed in the 1830s, but the first real computer, the UNIVAC I, was built in 1950. The computer filled a large room and did pretty much what an expensive hand-held calculator of today can do. At the time, people predicted that only a few computers would be needed because so little use could be made of the machines. Little did the early computer experts dream that, by the 1980s, thousands of computers would be sold every month. And these computers are not being sold just to scientists or engineers; they are being sold to people like you for use at home!

Computers today do what early computer experts never dreamed possible; they play colorful, animated games with lights and sounds. Some of the computers designed during the 1950s could play games such as checkers and chess.

Teaching the computer to play games was often done to help people learn better how to program the computer, just as playing games today can teach you more about your computer and how it works. The early games were played with a regular game board in front of the player. When a play was made, the name of the piece and the letter and number of the square to which that piece was to be moved would be typed into the computer. The computer would respond with the name of a piece and the letter and number of the square to which it was to be moved. There were no visual displays of pieces or moves. There were no interesting sounds when you won or lost a game. There were no flashing colors to tempt you to play. And there was no way to play if you weren't a computer expert or working with a computer expert.

How different computer games are today! And computers can be made to perform so many different tasks. Computers have grown so small that one can fit in a small case on your desk. They are being used for controlling household appliances and starting cars. They do tasks for businesses like keeping track of materials and sending out bills. They can do tasks for you. They can challenge you to learn how to write your own game programs. They can challenge you to write programs to use when you do your homework. They can challenge you to think up your own uses for the computer. You only need to know enough about how a computer works and how to program a computer to make the machine do what you want it to do.

Chapter 2
Plugs, Boards, Wire and Silicon

If someone asks you to describe a computer you would probably tell them about the parts that you can see: the case, the keyboard, the video screen. These three parts of a computer are called *hardware*. There are other types of hardware that can be connected to the computer. If you were to look inside the computer case you would find many more hardware components. You would see plugs, wires, boards and many small rectangular items. You could find similar items in other electronic devices; for example, in televisions and tape recorders. Although many of the components can be found in other devices, some special items are found in computers.

There are three major categories of special hardware needed to make a computer. They are the *central processing unit* or the CPU, *input/output* devices and *memory* or *storage* devices. The computer's video screen is an *output device*. It is an output device because the computer sends out information like letters or pictures to its screen. The keyboard is an *input device* because it is used to send information to the computer. The CPU and memory devices work together. They decide what to do with the information from the input devices. They decide what information to send to the output devices.

The CPU

In a microcomputer the CPU is a single integrated circuit. The integrated circuit is usually a black rectangle about 50 millimeters (mm) by 15mm. It looks a lot like a large centipede with about 40 metal legs. This small device makes all the decisions that a computer makes. A computer is not a computer without a CPU.

A pocket radio may have five or ten transistors in it. The CPU integrated circuit contains a very thin piece or "chip" of *silicon* that has thousands of microscopic transistors. Silicon is one of the 100 basic elements that make up the universe. This chip is about 5mm square. The transistors are connected to form many circuits.

The way that the circuits are hooked together determines how the CPU can work. Although there can be many different circuits in different CPU's there are some circuits that are found in all CPU's. Each CPU has registers, an arithmetic logic unit and control circuits. The *registers* store information. The *arithmetic logic unit* does arithmetic and makes decisions. It works with the information stored in the registers. The *control circuits* decide what jobs the arithmetic logic unit will do and when it should do them.

Input/Output Devices

While the CPU can perform many functions, it cannot communicate with you directly. It can communicate with other devices such as video screens and keyboards through interface circuits. These circuits convert the electrical signals that the CPU uses to electrical signals that the video screens or keyboards can use. The CPU communicates with the interface circuits over metal strips that are grouped together in what are called *busses.* There is a *data bus* which carries information to and from the CPU. There is an *address bus* which is used by the CPU to say which interface circuit it wants to talk with or address. There is also a *control bus* which is used by both the CPU and the interface circuits to make sure that only one operation takes place at a time. The CPU also uses the control bus to say that it only wants interface circuits to respond.

The interface circuits are connected to input/output or I/O

devices. The keyboard is an example of an input device. it sends information to the CPU. Other devices that are used only for input are the joysticks and buttons used with games. The video screen and printers are examples of output devices. They receive information from the CPU. Some devices are used for both input and output. An example is a modem. This device allows your microcomputer to communicate over the phone lines with another computer. Input and output devices can also be the equipment used in experiments or around the home. For example, the computer could be connected to a thermostat, an input device, and the controls for the furnace, an output device, to regulate and monitor the heating and cooling of a home.

Memory and Mass Storage

If you have a CPU and I/O connections you still do not have a computer. You must have some *memory* for the CPU to use. The CPU uses the memory as a place to store information. It also uses memory as the place to find out what to do. The CPU looks in memory for a *program*, a set of instructions on what to do. If it does not have a program in memory, all that a CPU can do is some meaningless operations. It cannot perform because there is no set of instructions to tell it what to do. The computer also looks in its memory for *data*, information with which to work.

You can think of memory as many mailboxes hooked together.

You can think of memory as many rows of mailboxes hooked together. Each box can hold one piece of information, or "mail". The information can be either an instruction in a program or a piece of data. Each box in the row has a name on it, or *address.* While there are not really mailboxes in memory the idea of specific, labeled, places to hold information is important. The CPU uses the labels or addresses to find information.

There are two types of memory, *main memory* and *mass storage.* Main memory is inside the computer. It consists of one or more integrated circuits, each containing a memory chip. Memory chips are a lot like the CPU chip. They are made of silicon and have thousands of transistors contained in a small space. They have different circuits than the CPU, but those circuits are similar to the registers of the CPU. Like the circuits of the registers, the circuits of memory chips are designed to store information.

There are two types of main memory, RAM and ROM. *RAM* stands for *Random Access Memory.* If you think about the mailboxes again you can understand what random access means. If you have ten mailboxes hooked together and if each box has a number, I can tell you to put somthing in box five and you can do it. You do not have to put something in boxes one, two, three and four before you put your item in box five. With random access memory the CPU can interact with any address or space directly. It does not have to go first to any other space. With RAM, the CPU can get information from an address or put information into it. We say that RAM is read/write memory.

ROM stands for *Read Only Memory* which is a special kind of RAM. ROM contains information that the CPU can "read" but cannot change. It is also different from RAM in another way. *ROM is permanent memory. Read/write RAM is temporary memory.* When you turn off your computer all the information in RAM is lost, but the information in ROM is not lost. ROM is important because when you turn on your computer there will be meaningful instructions for the CPU to follow. Some computers use plug-in ROM cartridges. They are still considered as part of main memory.

The CPU is connected to the memory using the same three busses that connect it to the I/O devices. The address bus says which space in memory the CPU wants to read or write. The control bus carries the information that the CPU only wants memory devices to respond and says whether the CPU wants to read or write. The data bus takes information to or from the memory.

Often when people work with computers they want to save the work they have done. They cannot save their work in RAM because when they turn the computer off RAM loses all its information. They cannot save their information in ROM because the computer cannot write to ROM. The work they have done can be saved in a special memory called *mass storage devices.*

There are several types of mass storage devices. For home microcomputers the most common is the cassette tape recorder. The information from RAM memory is recorded on the tape. The CPU directs an I/O device to change the memory information into tones that are then recorded. The I/O device can also change the tones back into information that the CPU can use. The tape recorder is not a random access device. If the CPU wants information that is stored near the middle of the tape, it has to read through all the information that comes before. This kind of memory is called *sequential memory.*

Another way of storing data is on disks. Information on disks is stored as magnetic fields. Disks are random accesss devices. The CPU can get information from any place on the disk without reading other information. To do this, it "plays" the disk on a disk drive. Because the disk is random access, it is faster for locating information than the cassette tape recorder. It is also able to send and receive the information faster than the cassette recorder can. Disks are somewhat more reliable than cassette recorders.

Other types of mass storage devices that are not usually used with home microcomputers are paper tapes and punch cards. People are working on other types of mass storage. One new type is the *bubble memory.* In this device,

16

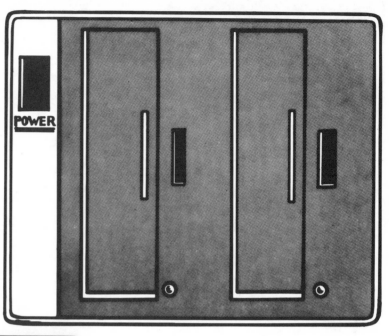

Power Disk Drive

Diskette

information is stored as very small magnetic regions in a crystal. People are also working on using video cassette recorders and video disks for mass storage.

Now if someone asks you to describe a computer you can tell them that the computer is more than a case, a keyboard, and a video screen. It is a CPU, input/output interfaces and devices, and RAM and ROM memory and mass storage.

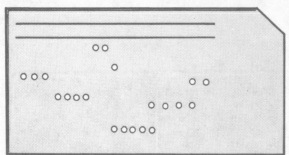

Punch Card

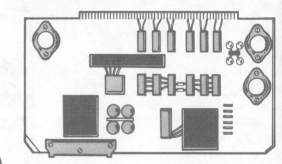

Board that plugs into computer with bubble memory modules.

Paper punch tape

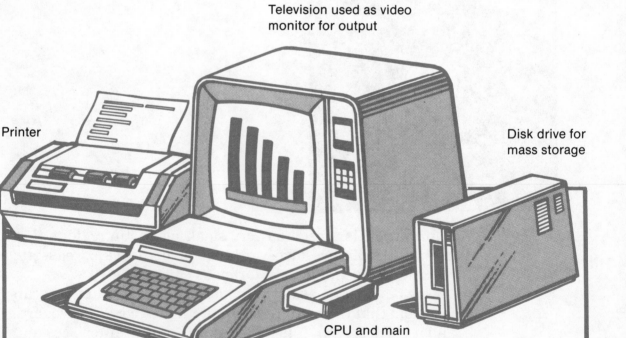

Television used as video monitor for output

Printer

Disk drive for mass storage

CPU and main memory

Keyboard for input

18

Chapter 3

Bits, Nibbles, Bytes and Words

Computer hardware is interesting but the hardware will just sit on your table and do nothing unless you can tell it what to do. Plugs, boards, wires and silicon can't play games or help you do your homework. You must tell the computer what to do. Computer *software* is used to tell the computer what to do.

Binary Numbers and Computers

The most primary way to tell a computer what to do is to use a system to put instructions directly in the computer's memory. You must give the memory your instructions. The CPU looks in its memory and finds your instructions in a way that they can be stored. The memory chips are like little switches. They can be either off or on. Computer people say that "off" is a 0 and that "on" is a 1. When people count using just the two numbers 0 and 1, they are using a *binary counting system,* or base two.

You usually count in base ten. You use the numbers 0, 1, 2, 3, 4, 5, 6, 7, 8, and 9. You write numbers over nine by using two or more of these numbers. You use 1 and 5 to write 15. Your computer uses just 0 and 1 to make numbers. Look at the way your computer counts.

```
0    is    0000
1    is    0001
2    is    0010
3    is    0011          '
4    is    0100
8    is    1000
15   is    1111
```

Each of the spaces filled by a 0 or a 1 is called a *bit.* A group of
four bits is called a *nibble.* The numbers 0 to 15 are each
represented by one nibble. Most computers group two nibbles together at one address or place in memory. These two
nibbles are called a *byte.*

If you wanted to count above 15 you could get confused
using just 0 and 1. You would have to put two or more nibbles
together and you would have a string made up of eight
numbers or more—all 0 or 1. Even if you didn't get confused
on the order of the numbers, you would soon get tired of
flipping switches.

Computer people wanted an easier way to tell the computer
what to do. They let the computer do some of the work. Using
the set of switches they wrote a program to tell the computer
how to read a set of buttons or keys to put the information
into memory. They then borrowed a system from mathemati-
cians to help them count larger numbers using only four bits
at a time. They use a number system based on numerals for 0
to 15, sixteen numbers in all. The system is called *hexadecimal* and uses the letters A, B, C, D, E and F for the five
numbers bigger than 9.

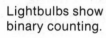

Lightbulbs show
binary counting.

0	is	0
5	is	5
9	is	9
10	is	A
11	is	B
12	is	C
13	is	D
14	is	E
15	is	F
16	is	10
20	is	14
30	is	1E

They could now label their buttons 0 to F. When they pressed a sequence of buttons they could tell the computer the information they wanted it to have without flipping switches.

1 2 3 4 5 6 7 8 9 0
A B C D E F

A 7-segment display shows the numbers and letters of HEX counting.

Using the hexadecimal keys to send information to the computer does not change the information the computer gets. You are just using a program to help you group the information so that you do not have to flip switches. You still are putting in bytes of information, but your computer is helping you.

21

Now you can see that eight bits are two nibbles and two nibbles are one byte. With one byte you can count from 0 to 255. In hexadecimal, 255 is FF. Bits in memory are grouped so that either eight, sixteen or thirty-two bits of information are at one address. The information at an address is called a word. Your computer probably uses either an 8-bit or a 16-bit word.

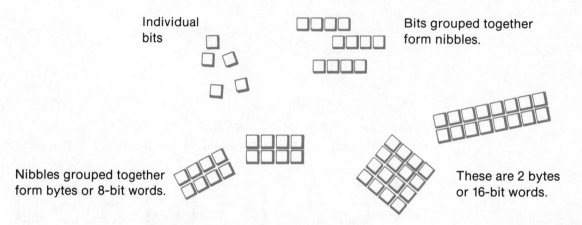

Individual bits

Bits grouped together form nibbles.

Nibbles grouped together form bytes or 8-bit words.

These are 2 bytes or 16-bit words.

The information which people would represent as a hexadecimal number is still a group of off-on signals for the computer. The computer reads the signals at an address and decides what it is being told to do. When your computer starts, it goes to an address in memory and gets whatever information is there. It assumes that the information is an instruction. The transistors inside the CPU know how to interpret the instructions. The CPU is designed to take a set of zeros and ones and interpret the set as a particular command. For different computers the same set of zeros and ones will stand for different instructions.

You can let the 255 numbers of one byte be 255 different instructions for the computer. Instruction 1 could mean: add two numbers and instruction 2 could mean: subtract two numbers. But 256 addresses are not enough places to store information a computer needs to do difficult tasks. To have more space for information, most computers use two bytes for an address. Using two bytes, they can have over 64,000 addresses for information.

Assembly Language

Computer people soon got tired of pushing the hexadecimal keys. They wrote a hexadecimal program to tell the computer how to interpret special words. Instead of giving the hexadecimal instruction for add, they could type in the word "add." The computer would decide that the word "add" meant to put a certain set of off-on commands at a certain address. Being able to program the computer using these simple words for instructions is called an *assembly language.* Assembly language was the first language to use words that people usually recognize for commands. It is not a complex language, but it is still used today even though more complex programming languages have been developed. Assembly language programming is used whenever you want a program that takes little space in memory or that needs only a little time to operate.

ADDING 2 + 3

BINARY PROGRAM
0010000100000000100000000
0011111000000011
11000110000000001001110111

HEXIDECIMAL PROGRAM
210100
3E03
C60277

ASSEMBLY PROGRAM
LXI H,0100H
MVI A,03H
ADI 02H
MOV M,A

Program Languages

DO YOU SPEAK BASIC?

When most people think of programming a computer they think of using a more complex language than assembly language. Many complex languages have been developed. For home computers, BASIC is the most common programming language. The complex languages let the computer programmer use a common word to stand for many assembly language instructions. For example, to add two numbers in BASIC you would write X=2+3. In assembly language you would need to use command words to tell the computer where to find the 2, to add the number 3 to it and where to put the answer. The BASIC language does all of the necessary steps with a single command.

Programming languages have special words to direct the computer to work with input and output devices. You can use the one word "PRINT" to tell the computer to put some information on your video screen. If you wanted to print to your screen in assembly language you would need to use several words. If you wanted to work in hexadecimal numbers, you would have to type in several hexadecimal numbers. If you wanted to work in binary numbers, you would have to flip many switches to the on or off positions.

The rest of this book will be talking about the words used in the BASIC language and how to put the words together to do something for you.

COMPUTER LANGUAGES

24

Chapter 4

Programming in BASIC

A computer program is a set of directions to a computer. Computer specialists have developed programming languages to make it easier to give a set of directions to the computer. You can learn to use your computer's BASIC language to instruct your computer to do what you want it to do. You need to learn to give the computer its instructions in the right order. You also have to start each direction to the computer on a line that begins with a number. In the programs that we help you write, we will use the numbers 10, 20, 30 etc. But before you begin to write statements to the computer, you need to know what you want to do. You need an idea.

Here is an example of a simple idea.

I want the computer to ask me my name and then print me a message that says "Hello."

Some BASIC Statements

Once you have an idea, you are ready to begin to write a program. You need to know about the format of a program and about some BASIC statements that will get the computer to do your task. BASIC sentences or "lines" are always written in the same format or pattern. You must always begin a line with a number. You should not number your lines 1, 2, 3, 4....You should number your lines 10, 20, 30, 40...or 100, 200, 300, 400....You number your lines by tens or bigger skips so that if you need to add a line to your program at some later time, you can add it with a number between those already in your program. You won't have to renumber all of your lines.

Another important format of lines is the way you write the orders you want to give your computer. The orders are also called *statements*. You should have your line number, a space made by hitting your space key, and the statement or order you want to use. If you want to put somthing else on a line you must put a space, a comma (,) or a semicolon (;) after your statement.

You can use the ideas about line format to write a line to name the program idea we wrote above:

I want the computer to ask me my name and then print me a message that says "Hello."

Let's call the program to do this job:

```
ASK MY NAME PROGRAM
```

REM Statement

A program should be given a name before you include any other statements. You can name your program on the very first line of the program by using a REM statement. REM is short for remark. It is a BASIC statement or order to your computer. But a remark line is really a line to tell you something. It orders your computer to skip all the rest of the words in the line or sentence. The statement to name your program looks like this:

```
10 REM ASK MY NAME PROGRAM
```

You can see that you should start the line with a number and that you should leave a space after the number before writing the statement. You should also set off any statements from other information on this line with a space. The REM statement above is really typed:

```
10[space]REM[space]ASK MY NAME PROGRAM
```

26

PRINT, INPUT, Variable Names and END

To write your program you need to know some other BASIC statements.* You need to learn about the PRINT statement. The PRINT statement tells the computer to type out whatever you tell it to print. Here is how the PRINT statement will look in your program to ask your name:

```
10 REM ASK MY NAME PROGRAM
20 PRINT ''WHAT IS YOUR NAME?''
```

You can see that the question that you want the computer to type is inside quotation marks (" "). Whenever you want the computer to type something you must put your words inside of quotation marks.

The next statement you need to know is the INPUT statement. The INPUT statement lets you tell the computer that you are going to give it some information from the keyboard. When we use an INPUT statement to tell the computer words like your name, we must tell the computer where to save the information. We use a single letter (some computers can use two letters or a letter and a number) and a $ symbol to name the word or group of words. The $ symbol tells the computer to look for a set of letters or numbers in a *string*—it is not getting a long number to add or multiply. It is getting a list of letters or a list of numbers to save in just the order in which they are typed. We will look at the INPUT statement more later and you will see more clearly the meaning of a string.

Look at our program when you add the INPUT statement:

```
10 REM ASK MY NAME PROGRAM
20 PRINT ''WHAT IS YOUR NAME?''
30 INPUT N$
```

The INPUT statement has the name of a location of a place in memory or a *variable* called N$. Do you know why it has the name N$? Because N is the first letter of the word name. The $ must come right after the letter. You must have the $ so the computer knows to look for a group or string of letters to save.

---

*The Appendix lists the Basic Statements for several computers. Check to see if information on your computer is included.

You need one more statement to make a complete program. You need the END statement. Some computers need the END statement to tell them that you are finished with the program. We will include it in our programs so that they can be used on the computers that need it.

Now your complete program looks like this:

```
10 REM ASK MY NAME PROGRAM
20 PRINT ''WHAT IS YOUR NAME?''
30 INPUT N$
40 END
```

Now you are ready to write your program. With your computer set up to work in BASIC, type in the statements just as they are written above. Now you are ready to use the command RUN to make the computer do what your program tells it to!

When you type in RUN you should see

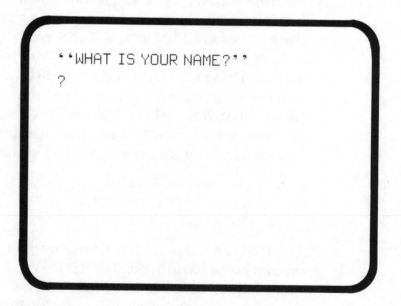

The second ? is a *prompt.* A prompt is used by the computer to let you know that it is waiting for you to type in the information for which it has asked. You should now type in your name. The computer may come back with the word OK. OK is another prompt to tell you that it has finished running your program.

You can now add to your program and make the computer use your name in a message that says "Hello." We will use the PRINT statement again. We will also need to move our END statement. Look at the new lines we will need to add:

```
40 PRINT ''HELLO'', N$
50 PRINT ''I LIKE TO TALK TO YOU.''
60 END
```

Look carefully at line 40. We used the quote marks around the word we wanted to print. Then we had to use a comma to tell the computer to look for something else to print. That something else is the information it saved in the variable called N$. You know that your name is in N$!

Now you have a program to do what we wanted to do. We have taken an idea and written statements to make the computer follow our directions. Our idea was:

I want the computer to ask me my name and then print me a message that says "Hello."

Here is the program all together:

```
10 REM ASK MY NAME PROGRAM
20 PRINT ''WHAT IS YOUR NAME?''
30 INPUT N$
40 PRINT ''HELLO'', N$
50 PRINT ''I LIKE TO TALK TO YOU.''
60 END
```

Now you can RUN our program. This is what you should see on your screen:

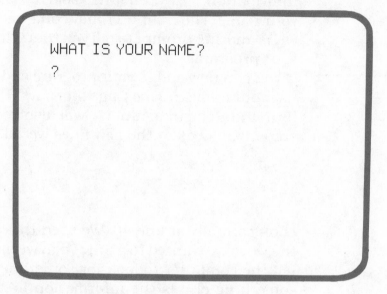

```
WHAT IS YOUR NAME?
?
```

You should type in your name. Let's pretend your name is PAT. Type in PAT. You will see

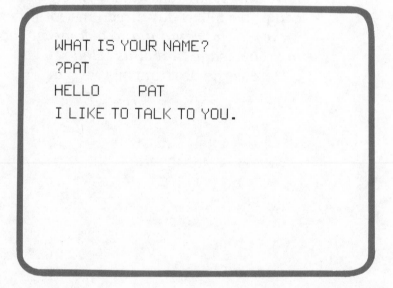

```
WHAT IS YOUR NAME?
?PAT
HELLO     PAT
I LIKE TO TALK TO YOU.
```

Now that you know how to use the INPUT and PRINT statements you can write other simple programs. Why not have the computer ask you your name and the name of your best friend? Your program idea sentence might be:

I want the computer to type out my name and the name of my best friend.

You could use the variable F$ for your best friend's name. Here is how your program might look:

```
10 REM MY FRIEND AND I
20 PRINT "WHAT IS YOUR NAME?"
30 INPUT N$
40 PRINT "HELLO", N$
50 PRINT "WHAT IS THE NAME OF YOUR BEST FRIEND?"
60 INPUT F$
70 PRINT "NOW I KNOW THAT YOUR BEST FRIEND IS", F$
80 END
```

You can use these statements to have your computer repeat back to you any other kind of information you want. You just need to have an INPUT statement and a variable name for whatever information you want the computer to print.

GOTO, "Comma", "Semicolon"

How would you like to fill up your screen with your name? You can use BASIC statements to make your computer print your name many times. Your program idea sentence would be:

I want the computer to print my name over and over.

You would use the statement GOTO. The GOTO statement tells the computer to go find a line in your program and do what that line tells it to do. You remember the program for having the computer print you a message. It went like this:

```
10 REM ASK MY NAME PROGRAM
20 PRINT "WHAT IS YOUR NAME?"
30 INPUT N$
40 PRINT "HELLO", N$
50 PRINT "I LIKE TO TALK TO YOU."
60 END
```

We can change this program to do our new task. Look at the changes and the new lines:

```
10 REM PRINT MY NAME MANY TIMES PROGRAM
20 PRINT ''WHAT IS YOUR NAME?''
30 INPUT N$
40 PRINT N$
50 GOTO 40
60 END
```

You can see that the computer will now only print your name. It does not have instructions to print anything else. You also see that line 50 now says "GOTO 40". We are telling the computer to go back to line 40 and do what that line tells it to do. Line 40 tells the computer to print your name. The computer will keep printing your name until you tell it to stop! How do you tell it to stop? You use the key labeled "BREAK" or "STOP" or you use the "CONTROL" key and the "C" key. You have to tell the computer to stop running your program to have it stop printing your name. Do you see why? Every time the computer goes back to line 40 it then goes to line 50. Line 50 sends it back to line 40. The computer never makes it to the END statement!

You should type in this new program and see your computer keep printing your name. If your name were PAT, your screen will look like the one below until it is full and then the lines at the top will disappear and only your name will be on the screen.

```
WHAT IS YOUR NAME?
?
PAT
PAT
PAT
PAT
PAT
PAT
PAT
PAT
PAT
PAT
PAT
PAT
PAT
```

You can change this program to print any word or sentence over and over. You just need to change line 20 to ask you for new information. Just remember that to stop the words you must use a control (C) or a stop or break key.

Your name has been printed only once on each line. You can make a simple change that will make the computer print your name on a line more than once. You can use a comma (,) or a semicolon (;) in line 40. Look at line 40 with a comma:

```
40 Print N$,
```

The comma comes right after N$. The comma tells the computer to print whatever is in N$ on the line on your screen and not to go to the next line until the line it is on is full. It also tells the computer to print the information in *fields* or groups of spaces. If your name is shorter than the number of spaces in the field that your computer uses, you will have blank spaces in front of your name. Type in the new line 40 and run your program. You will see this on your screen:

```
WHAT IS YOUR NAME?
?
        PAT     PAT     PAT     PAT
        PAT     PAT     PAT     PAT
        PAT     PAT     PAT     PAT
        PAT     PAT     PAT     PAT
        PAT     PAT     PAT     PAT
        PAT     PAT     PAT     PAT
        PAT     PAT     PAT     PAT
        PAT     PAT     PAT     PAT
        PAT     PAT     PAT     PAT
        PAT     PAT     PAT     PAT
        PAT     PAT     PAT     PAT
        PAT     PAT     PAT     PAT
        PAT     PAT     PAT     PAT
```

If you use a semicolon (;) in place of the comma in line 40, you will get a new pattern. The computer will repeat writing your name without putting in any spaces. It will fill a line on your screen with your name, each name touching the name next to it. Then you really can fill the screen with your name!

```
WHAT IS YOUR NAME
?
PATPATPATPATPATPATPATPATPATPATPAT
PATPATPATPATPATPATPATPATPATPATPAT
PATPATPATPATPATPATPATPATPATPATPAT
PATPATPATPATPATPATPATPATPATPATPAT
```

You must always remember to hit the "BREAK" or "STOP" key or the "CONTROL C" when you want to stop your program. But maybe you want to have the computer repeat your name only a few times and then stop by itself. You can use two new orders that go together. The statements are FOR and NEXT.

FOR, NEXT FOR tells the computer to do whatever the lines after the FOR line say to do. When you write a FOR statement, you must also tell the computer how many times it must repeat the statement. You tell the computer to count the times it does the job. You must give the computer some place in memory to store its count. We used a variable name to tell the computer where to store information when we used an INPUT statement. We also use a variable name when we use a FOR statement. However, there is a difference in the variables. Our INPUT variable was a string variable; that is, it was a string of letters to be saved as a string. Our FOR variable is a number. It is the number of times the computer has done the task. It gets bigger every time the computer does our job. We do not save the number as a string but as a number. When we have a number variable we name it with a letter but we do not use a "$." Computer programmers often

35

use J or K as the name of the counter variable. We tell the computer to count from 1 to whatever number of times we want our task completed. Here is how your statement would look:

```
35 FOR J=1 TO 5
```

The computer knows to do whatever comes next for 5 times. But you have not told it what to do. The lines that come after this line tell the computer what to do. So:

```
35 FOR J=1 TO 5
40 PRINT N$
```

Now you have told the computer to print N$ on your screen 5 times. But your computer is looking for more lines of things to do. It keeps looking for lines of jobs until it finds a NEXT statement. The NEXT statement tells the computer that it has done all the jobs it needs to do. The NEXT statement needs to tell the computer the variable it is using as a counter so the computer will know what FOR goes with the NEXT statement. Here is the program to tell the computer to type your name 5 times, once on each line:

```
10 REM ASK MY NAME PROGRAM
20 PRINT ''WHAT IS YOUR NAME?''
30 INPUT N$
35 FOR J=1 TO 5
40 PRINT N$
50 NEXT J
60 END
```

You can try using FOR-NEXT loops to print more than one item in the same program. You just need to be sure to have a FOR line, the line of what you want printed, and then your NEXT line. And remember that the FOR line and the NEXT line must have the same variable for their counters.

LET and Doing Arithmetic

The LET statement lets you do arithmetic in your programs. You can use LET to add, subtract, multiply and divide numbers. You use LET with a number variable, a single letter that can stand for a number. You remember that number variables have a letter and no $ for their name. A program for counting by twos, fives or tens will show you how to use the LET statement. The program also uses the other statements you have learned.

```
10 REM COUNTING BY TWOS, FIVES OR TENS
20 PRINT ''DO YOU WANT TO COUNT BY TWOS, FIVES OR TENS?''
30 PRINT ''TYPE IN 2, 5, or 10.''
40 INPUT N
50 LET C=0
60 FOR J=1 TO 10
70 LET C=C+N
80 PRINT C
90 NEXT J
100 END
```

Line 50 sets your variable C as 0 so that your program begins counting at zero. The statement says that C is now zero. On line 70 the LET statement is being used to let you add. When you count by twos you are really just adding two to each number that you have. Counting by twos is really saying 0+2=2, 2+2=4, 4+2=6...Line 70 tells the computer to do the same thing but it tells it to do the task with variables. Because the program has variables, you can count by twos or by fives or tens—you count by whatever number you type in when the computer asks for the variable N. The FOR-NEXT loop lets you count out ten numbers. Try doing other kinds of counting like counting by threes or sixes. You can even count backwards by these numbers! You only have to change line 50 to

```
50 LET C=100 [or some other large number]
```

and change line 70 to

```
70 LET C=C-N
```

You can also write simple programs to print out the answers to arithmetic problems. Here is a program to let you do some simple multiplication (The symbol * is used):

```
10 REM MULTIPLICATION PROGRAM
```

```
20 FOR J=1 TO 5
30 PRINT ''GIVE ME THE FIRST NUMBER''
40 INPUT N
50 PRINT ''GIVE ME THE SECOND NUMBER''
60 INPUT M
70 LET C=N*M
80 PRINT C
90 NEXT J
100 END
```

The LET statement lets you take the result of your arithmetic work and save the number in a place in memory. When you say LET C=C+2 you are saying take what is stored in memory at the place called C, add the number two and store the new number in the same place in memory. Then you can use a PRINT statement to have the number stored in C printed on your screen.

IF-THEN Statements

There is one last set of statements that you need to know to write simple BASIC programs.* Those statements are the IF and THEN statements. These two statements allow your computer to make decisions. When your computer sees these statements it knows it must decide what to do with the information it has. These two statements must always be used together and they must always be used with some other information. You must tell the computer that IF something is true, THEN do something. You can use an IF-THEN statement in the program for counting by twos, fives and tens. Here is how the program will look:

```
10 REM COUNTING BY TWOS, FIVES OR TENS
20 PRINT ''DO YOU WANT TO COUNT BY TWOS, FIVES OR TENS?''
30 PRINT ''TYPE IN 2, 5, OR 10.''
40 INPUT N
41 REM NEXT 5 LINES CHECK IF N IS OK
```

*Check the Appendix for information on the Texas Instruments computer.

```
42 IF N=2 THEN GOTO 50
43 IF N=5 THEN GOTO 50
44 IF N=10 THEN GOTO 50
45 PRINT ''PLEASE, 2, 5, OR 10 ONLY''
46 GOTO 40
47 REM WE REACH LINE 50 ONLY FOR OK N
50 LET C=0
60 FOR J=1 TO 10
70 LET C=C+N
80 PRINT C
90 NEXT J
100 END
```

The IF-THEN statement is used with the equals symbol (=) to say IF the response is what the computer wants, THEN it is ok to do the next part of the statement. If the IF part is not what the computer wants, then it skips over the THEN part of the statement and goes on to the next line of the program. IF-THEN is used to check to see if the correct number for the program has been entered. The IF-THEN statement can also be used to see if strings are just as they are to be written. When IF-THEN is used to check on a string, the string must be inside quote marks (" "). Here is a simple program to check on a string in the name program:

```
10 REM CHECK TO SEE IF KNOW YOU
20 PRINT ''WHAT IS YOUR NAME?''
30 INPUT N$
40 IF N$=''PAT'' THEN PRINT ''HELLO, I KNOW YOU''
50 IF N$=''PAT'' THEN GOTO 70
60 PRINT ''YOU ARE A NEW FRIEND'' ,N$
70 END
```

The IF-THEN can be used with the symbols < (less than) and > (greater than) just like it is used with the equals symbol. Also, almost any statement can come after the THEN. You can say THEN PRINT or THEN GOTO or THEN INPUT or THEN LET. Usually you can *not* say THEN FOR to start a FOR-NEXT loop or THEN END to get out of your program.

Now you know how to use some of the most important

statements in BASIC. You need to check your computer manual to find out how to do two other important tasks: how to load a program and how to save a program. The owner's guide for your computer will tell you how to save and load programs from your cassette recorder or disk drive. You will need to use these commands when you work on the longer programs in the next chapter and when you begin to write many of your own programs.

Chapter 5

Programs to Use and Change

Now you know most of the statements in BASIC that are used to write programs. You are ready to try some more complex programs. The programs in this chapter can help you with homework, drills and arithmetic facts. They can even show you how to have fun drawing pictures.

The programs here can be changed to perform in different ways. We will show you how to change some of the statement lines to make the program do different tasks. You may then want to use parts of our programs to design your own programs.*

The programs will be presented in blocks of numbered statements which will come after comments on what the statements do. When you are entering a program into your computer, you will need to type in the numbered lines just as they are written here. Always check for errors when you type in a line. If your program does not run, go back and check each line to see that it is just like the line in the book.

*Check the Appendix for information on using the programs with specific computers.

ROLLIT Program

The first program is called ROLLIT. This program will "roll a die" just as you do in a game. The program will roll a die as many times as you want it to. It will count how many times each number is "on top." We have included this program first so that you can learn a new concept. That concept is the concept of a *BASIC function*. We will use these functions in several programs. The first function is RND which stands for *random*. Random means that something happens by chance.

Random Numbers

This program comes up with random numbers between one and six. You cannot make one number come up consistently. The computer controls the number. If you "roll the die" many times, you will find that all the numbers come up about the same number of times.

Our program idea for the ROLLIT program is:

I want the computer to roll a die. I want it to ask me how many times to roll it. I want it to keep track of how many times I get any number.

The first part of the program gives the name of the program and asks you to tell how many times to roll the die. "T" is used as a variable for how many times you want to roll. Here is the first part of the program:

```
10 REM PROGRAM ROLL-IT
20 PRINT "HOW MANY TIMES DO YOU WANT TO ROLL?"
30 INPUT T
40 PRINT "HERE WE GO..."
```

The second part of the program tells the computer the numbers it will need to do some calculations later in the program. "L" will be the lowest number we want. The lowest number on a die is 1. "H" will be the highest number we want. The highest number on a die is six. We will use LET statements to tell the computer the lowest and highest numbers. "N" will be the number we roll each time we repeat the main part of the program. So we will have the computer roll the die to come up with a random number between one and six which it will save as "N1" to "N6." Every time the computer finds a one, it will make "N1" larger by one. Every time it finds a two, it will make "N2" larger by one. In this way it will keep track of the times the numbers one to six appear. Do you know what we will use to repeat our rolls a number of times? We will use a FOR loop. Here is the second part of the program:

```
50 LET L=1
60 LET H=6
70 FOR J=1 TO T
```

You need to learn another new BASIC function to tell the computer to produce random numbers that are *whole numbers.* If you do not tell the computer about the type of number you want it will express the numbers in decimals like 2.5673. You know that a die has only whole numbers and you want only whole numbers from the computer. The functions used to tell the computer to produce whole numbers is *INT* which stands for *integer.* The word integer means whole number. Here is the line to produce integers:

```
80 N=INT((H-L+1)*RND(1))+L
```

In the line above, RND(1) produces a number between zero and a little less than one. The (1) tells the computer to start a random set of numbers and go to the next random number in the set the next time the program asks for a new number. If you had a (0), the computer would always use the same number every time the program asked for a new number. You could not tell the computer which number to pick but once it picked that number it would not pick another one. You can see that the (1) is very important! The expression (H−L+1)*RND(1) gives a number between 0 and a little bit less than 6. You can see that this expression in this program is really (6−1+1)*RND(1) or 6*RND(1). Because RND (1) is never exactly 1, 6 times RND(1) will always be less than 6. In fact, the INT makes the number produced by the computer into 0, 1, 2, 3, 4, or 5. So how do we get the number 6? The last part of the line, the +L, tells the computer to add its number between 0 and 5 to the lowest number, which for this program is 1. Then we have a whole number between 1 and 6.

We now need to have statements to keep track of how many of each number the computer makes and to tell the computer to print out the results. To tell the computer how to keep track of the numbers we need to use IF statements. We need one IF statement for each of the six numbers on the die. To tell the computer to print out the results, we use PRINT statements. You probably remember that a NEXT statement is needed to close the FOR loop. Here are the statements:

```
90 IF N=1 THEN LET N1=N1+1
100 IF N=2 THEN LET N2=N2+1
110 IF N=3 THEN LET N3=N3+1
120 IF N=4 THEN LET N4=N4+1
130 IF N=5 THEN LET N5=N5+1
140 IF N=6 THEN LET N6=N6+1
150 NEXT J
160 PRINT : PRINT
170 PRINT ''WITH '';T;'' ROLLS OF THE DIE WE HAD''
180 PRINT ''1      '';N1;'' TIMES''
190 PRINT ''2      '';N2;'' TIMES''
200 PRINT ''3      '';N3;'' TIMES''
210 PRINT ''4      '';N4;'' TIMES''
220 PRINT ''5      '';N5;'' TIMES''
230 PRINT ''6      '';N6;'' TIMES''
240 END
```

You can run this program rolling the die 10 times or 50 times or several hundred times and see the difference in the results.

Program Arrays and DIM Statement

There is an easier way than using IF statements to keep track of the numbers rolled. You can use an *array*. An array is an organization of numbers or symbols. Arrays can be used in many ways. They are used to keep track of numbers while a computer is completing a FOR loop, or when the computer is working with more than one number, or when it is working with symbols that are similar. In this program, the computer is keeping track of numbers on the die. It needs to be able to change the number of times each shows up and to tell them apart. An array is just a different kind of variable, an *array*

variable. It requires a DIM statement, or *dimension statement,* to tell the computer how many items will be on the list. In the ROLLIT program, there are six numbers which we will call "F" for face. The dimension statement would be:

```
65 DIM F(6)
```

The (6) tells the computer that there are six faces, or numbers, to the die. F(1) stores the number of ones rolled. F(2) holds the number of twos; F(6), the number of sixes. You can rewrite the ROLLIT program using the array this way:

```
10 REM PROGRAM ROLL-IT
20 PRINT ''HOW MANY TIMES DO YOU WANT TO ROLL?''
30 INPUT T
40 PRINT ''HERE WE GO...''
50 LET L=1
60 LET H=6
65 DIM F(6)
70 FOR J=1 TO T
80 N=INT((H-L+1)*RND(1))+L
90 LET F(N)=F(N)+1
150 NEXT J
160 PRINT : PRINT
170 PRINT ''WITH'';T;'' ROLLS OF THE DIE WE HAD''
180 FOR J=1 TO 6
190 PRINT J;''   '';F(J);''   TIMES''
200 NEXT J
210 END
```

Program MATH

GOSUB

The next program is a program to help you drill your arithmetic facts. This program uses the random number function that you learned about in the ROLLIT program. It also uses the BASIC statement GOSUB. GOSUB sends the computer to a set of lines that have some directions for the computer. A GOSUB lets the computer skip to some lines at the end of the program. The group of lines is called a *subroutine.* When the computer completes the operations called for by the subroutine, it returns to the line after the GOSUB line. Subroutines often have large line numbers and are placed at the end of the program. When you have typed in the rest of the program, you will need to type in the subroutine.

To be able to write the MATH program you need to have a program idea. The program idea is:

I want to have the computer give me math problems from any one set of facts such as sixes or tens or twelves. I want the computer to tell me if my answers are right. I want it to give me three chances to get a correct answer. If I am not correct after three tries, I want the computer to tell me the right answer. I want to be able to change my program to do addition, subtraction, multiplication or division.

The first statements in the program tell the computer the information on the type of problems you want to do. The first lines are:

```
10 REM   PROGRAM MATH
20 LET O$=''A''
30 LET RA=12
40 LET FA=12
50 GOSUB 1000
```

The variable O$ is the variable to tell the computer what type of arithmetic you want to do. We set O$ equal to "A" because we have written the program to do addition. You can guess what letters you would use to do the other arithmetic operations—"S" is for SUBTRACTION, "M" is for MULTIPLICATION and "D" is for DIVISION. But how does the computer know what the letters stand for? You have to tell it and that is what the subroutine does. Line 50, GOSUB 1000, tells the computer to look at the lines starting at line 1000 and do what they say. They are lines to tell the computer what the "A," "S," "M," and "D" mean.

Line 30 tells the computer the largest number that can be used in the problems it gives you. We will use this variable, RA, to tell the computer that the random numbers it produces must always be 12 or less. (You can change RA to any number you choose to have the computer give you easier or harder problems.) Line 40 tells the computer that all the problems will be facts of twelve. This means that the computer will always drill you on the facts for whatever number you put into the expression FA=??. You can see that it is easy to change the program to drill you on any set of facts by changing this one line.

The next line tells the computer to find a random number that is a whole number between 0 and the value of RA.

```
80 LET N=INT((RA+1)*RND(1))
```

Because division is a somewhat different operation than addition, subtraction and multiplication, we need different directions for division. We need to have a way to include the lines for division so that the computer can do them when you want to do division. The next set of lines are for division only. The first line tells the computer to skip the division lines if the operation you want, 0$, is not "D."

```
90 IF 0$ <> ''D'' THEN GOTO 140
100 LET AN=N
110 LET N=AN*FA
130 GOTO 180
```

The GOTO statement tells the computer to skip lines 100, 110 and 130 if you want to do addition, subtraction or multiplication. The next lines tell the computer to do the correct operation for the letter you include in line 20.

```
140 IF 0$=''A'' THEN LET AN=FA+N
150 IF 0$=''S'' THEN LET AN=FA-N
160 IF 0$=''M'' THEN LET AN=FA*N
```

The variable AN stands for answer. These lines are calculating answers for the problems the computer gives you. If the computer does not calculate the answer, it cannot tell you if the answer you give is right or wrong. The next set of lines do just that—they give you a problem, look at your answer, check to see if you have given the correct answer, and keep track of how many times you have tried to answer the problem. The variable WR is used to keep track of how many times you have tried the problem. The variable X$ is taken from the subroutine that you will see later. The extra lines that just say PRINT are used to give you some space on the screen so it is easy to see the problem.

```
180 LET WR=0
190 PRINT
200 PRINT
210 PRINT
220 PRINT ''TRY THIS '';X$;'' PROBLEM:''
230 PRINT
240 IF O$=''D'' THEN PRINT N;'' '';Y$;'' '';FA
250 IF O$<>''D'' THEN PRINT FA;'' '';Y$;'' '';N
260 INPUT X
270 IF X=AN THEN PRINT ''VERY GOOD''
280 IF X=AN THEN GOTO 360
290 WR=WR+1
300 IF WR<>3 THEN PRINT ''THAT IS NOT CORRECT, TRY AGAIN''
310 IF WR<>3 THEN GOTO 230
320 PRINT ''THAT IS NOT CORRECT. THE CORRECT ANSWER IS:''
330 PRINT
```

The next set of lines are used only when you miss the problem three times. They tell you the problem and the correct answer.

```
340 IF O$=''D'' THEN PRINT N;'' '';Y$;'' '';FA;'' = '';AN
350 IF O$<>''D'' THEN PRINT FA;'' '';Y$;'' '';FA;'' = '';AN
360 PRINT
370 PRINT ''TRY ANOTHER PROBLEM''
380 GOTO 80
```

The following lines are the subroutine that you have been hearing so much about. This subroutine really doesn't do much, but it lets you know the type of problem you will be solving without your having to list the program. When you run the program, the subroutine will give the computer the correct word to put in a print statement that tells you the type of problem. The lines in the subroutine also introduce a new idea. The lines have more than one statement. There are two statements on each IF line. Including the two statements on a line means that you do not have to repeat the IF statement on a second line like we did in lines 300 and 310. You can see that the statements are separated by a colon (:). Notice that the subroutine starts with a remark line that identifies the next set of lines as a subroutine. The subroutine ends with line 1050 that says RETURN. A subroutine always ends with a RETURN statement.

```
1000 REM SUBROUTINE TO SET UP STRINGS FOR PRINTING
1010 IF O$="A" THEN LET X$="ADDITION":LET Y$="+"
1020 IF O$="S" THEN LET X$="SUBTRACTION":LET
     Y$="-"
1030 IF O$="M" THEN LET X$="MULTIPLICATION":LET
     Y$="*"
1040 IF O$="D" THEN LET X$="DIVISION":LET Y$="/"
1050 RETURN
```

The program needs one more line, the final line:

```
1060 END
```

When you run the program just as we have written it, you will do addition facts for twelve. You will have to use a control C or the break key to stop the program.

It is easy to change this program to review any group of facts or problems. You only have to change two lines. You change line 40 to change the type of facts you do. You change line 30 to tell the computer to give you easier or harder problems. You could also change the "VERY GOOD" in line 270 to some other comment that tells you that your answer is right. Maybe you want fewer or more chances to get the correct answer. Then you would change lines 300 and 310 to the number of chances you want. Maybe you want the computer to print your name when it gives you a problem. Then you must include the program from Chapter 4 in this program. You might want to include it as a subroutine.

Program LEARN

LEARN is a program that can help you whenever you have to learn some information that can be fit into multiple-choice questions. The multiple-choice format is a format like this:

Who was the first president of the USA?

a. Thomas Jefferson

b. George Washington

c. John Adams

The question is asked and you have to choose the one correct answer from three answers. The LEARN Program will let you write any questions you want but you will also need to know the right answers! You must tell the computer the correct answer and two incorrect answers. It will give you the three answers in random order. Here are the idea sentences for this program:

I want the computer to give me questions and three answer choices in random order for each question. The questions should also be given in random order. If I choose the correct answer, I want the computer to tell me I am correct. If I give the wrong answer, I want the computer to give me two chances.

This program uses arrays that were introduced earlier. It also uses a new function and two new statements. These new items are used in a subroutine. You will learn about them when you type in the subroutine. Here is the beginning of the program:

```
10 REM   PROGRAM LEARN
20 REM   PLACE QUESTIONS AND ANSWERS IN DATA STATEMENTS
30 DIM Q$(30),R$(30),S$(30),T$(30)
40 GOSUB 1000
```

You can see that there is an extra remark statement at the beginning of the program. The remark statement is there to remind you to enter your questions and answers at the end of the program.

Line 30 sets up the arrays to hold the questions and answers. The (30) after each variable name tells the computer that it needs space for thirty question and answer sets. You can easily change this number to show how many question sets you will really include—just be sure that you do not run out of memory! Q$(n) holds the question you want to ask. (n) stands for the particular question you want to ask, question 1, question 2 or question 30. R$(n) is an array to hold the

50

correct answer to your question. S$(n) and T$(n) hold the two incorrect answers.

The next line is a random number line and is used to decide which question to ask, your question 1 or your question 30. The lines that follow it are similar to the lines we used in the MATH programs to have the questions and answers printed on the screen. These lines also check to see if your answer is right or wrong.

```
50 LET Q=INT((N-1+1)*RND(1))+1
60 GOSUB 700
70 LET WR=0
80 PRINT:PRINT:PRINT
90 PRINT ''HERE COMES A QUESTION.........''
100 PRINT:PRINT:PRINT
110 PRINT Q$(Q)
120 PRINT ''A) '';A$
130 PRINT ''B) '';B$
140 PRINT ''C) '';C$
150 PRINT
160 INPUT ''THE CORRECT ANSWER IS...'';X$
170 IF X$=W$ THEN PRINT ''VERY GOOD!!!!''': GOTO 230
180 LET WR=WR+1
190 IF WR<>2 THEN PRINT ''THAT IS NOT CORRECT, TRY AGAIN'':
    GOTO 100
200 PRINT ''THAT IS NOT CORRECT, THE CORRECT ANSWER IS:''
210 PRINT:PRINT
220 PRINT W$;'') '';R$(Q)
230 PRINT:PRINT
240 PRINT ''TRY ANOTHER PROBLEM......''
250 GOTO 50
```

The next part of the program is a subroutine to allow the computer to decide in which order the answers to a particular question should be given. You will recognize the random number lines that let the computer use a random number to decide the order of the answers.

```
700 REM SUBROUTINE ON ORDER TO GIVE RESPONSES
710 REM NEED THE NUMBERS 1, 2, 3, IN RANDOM ORDER
```

```
720 LET P=INT((3-1+1)*RND(1))+1
730 LET P1=INT((3-1+1)*RND(1))+1
740 IF P1=P THEN GOTO 730
750 IF P< >1 AND P1< >1 THEN LET P2=1
760 IF P< >2 AND P1< >2 THEN LET P2=2
770 IF P< >3 AND P1< >3 THEN LET P2=3
780 IF P=1 THEN LET A$=R$(Q)
790 IF P=2 THEN LET A$=S$(Q)
800 IF P=3 THEN LET A$=T$(Q)
810 IF P1=1 THEN LET B$=R$(Q)
820 IF P1=2 THEN LET B$=S$(Q)
830 IF P1=3 THEN LET B$=T$(Q)
840 IF P2=1 THEN LET C$=R$(Q)
850 IF P2=2 THEN LET C$=S$(Q)
860 IF P2=3 THEN LET C$=T$(Q)
870 IF P=1 THEN LET W$=''A''
880 IF P1=1 THEN LET W$=''B''
890 IF P2=1 THEN LET W$=''C''
900 RETURN
```

READ and DATA Statements

The next subroutine introduces the READ and DATA statements and the LEFT$ function. The READ statement tells the computer to look through the program and find some DATA statements. The DATA statements have some information that the computer needs to use. The READ statement is like the INPUT statement except that the computer gets its information from the DATA statement rather than from the keyboard. The LEFT$ function lets the computer look at part of a string of characters. As you might guess from the name, it lets the computer look at the characters starting on the left. You must tell the computer which string to review and just how many characters to consider. There is a special way to tell the computer this information. After LEFT$ you use a "(" and then give the variable name of the string. Next, you need a comma (,) and a number to tell the computer how many characters to consider. You then need a ")". The function line is always written in this format. You will see this function in line 1030. We use the LEFT$ function so that the computer can find a special symbol that tells the computer that the last

question has been read. For our program we have used **. We
need to tell the computer when it has come to the last question so it can keep track of the number of questions.

```
1000 REM SUBR TO READ IN QUESTIONS AND RESPONSES
1010 LET N=1
1020 READ Q$(N)
1030 IF LEFT$(Q$(N),2)=''**'' THEN GOTO 1100
1040 REM   IN ABOVE CHECK IF AT END YET
1050 READ R$(N)
1060 READ S$(N)
1070 READ T$(N)
1080 LET N=N+1
1090 GOTO 1020
1100 REM   HERE WHEN ALL DONE
1110 LET N=N-1
1140 RETURN
```

The next statements are the DATA statements that the
computer reads. We have included a simple set of DATA statements so you can see the format in which the statements
must be written. The line number is followed by the statement DATA and a space. The information is placed inside
quote marks because they are strings like the strings that
often follow a PRINT statement. For this program you must
always type in the question, the correct answer and the two
incorrect answers.

```
10000  REM PUT DATA STATEMENTS HERE
10010  DATA ''WHICH OF THE FOLLOWING IS A TYPE OF CAR''
10020  DATA ''FORD''
10030  DATA ''ROBIN''
10040  DATA ''MACK''
10050  DATA ''IN WHAT COUNTRY WAS THIS BOOK WRITTEN''
10060  DATA ''UNITED STATES OF AMERICA''
10070  DATA ''CHICAGO''
10080  DATA ''WISCONSIN''
10090  DATA ''WHAT IS THE 8*9''
10100  DATA ''72''
```

```
10110 DATA ''81''
10120 DATA ''56''
10130 DATA ''A BASIC OUTPUT STATEMENT IS''
10140 DATA ''PRINT''
10150 DATA ''REM''
10160 DATA ''INPUT''
10170 DATA ''CUP STANDS FOR''
10180 DATA ''CENTRAL PROCESSING UNIT''
10190 DATA ''CENTRAL PENNSLYVANIA UNIVERSITY''
10200 DATA ''CIVIL POLICE UNIT''
11000 DATA *********
11010 REM USE ABOVE AS FLAG TO KNOW WHEN TO QUIT
11020 END
```

Notice that line 10010 is the question statement. Line 10020 is the correct answer and lines 10030 and 10040 are the incorrect answers for the first question. You can write any questions you want, but you must always have a line for the question, a line for the correct answer and two lines for the incorrect answers.

MOVEIT Program

The MOVEIT program is another program that uses the random function. The program introduces the idea of controlling where to put information on the screen. This technique is called, *cursor control.* The program will let you move the cursor around to place some character on the screen. This program may need to be changed to work on your computer. Different computers use different commands to do the tasks that are done in this program. The appendix lists the special characters or statements that a number of computers use. If your computer is not included, you can find a list of characters in your computer manual.

Our computer clears the screen with a control-L. A control-L is stored in the computer as a number, the number 12. A special function is used to store the number. That function is CHR$ which stands for character$. The function is followed by (12), the number for a clear screen. The function tells the computer to produce a string one character long. The character is the character represented by the number in the

54

I FEEL CLEAR AGAIN!

parenthesis, in this case a control-L. See what happens when you enter the statement:

```
PRINT CHR$(72);CHR$(69);CHR$(76);CHR$(79)
```

Either your computer will tell you that you have given it some information it does not understand or it will put some letters on your screen. If your computer seems not to like this procedure, check in the appendix for some additional information.

The idea sentence for MOVEIT is:

I want the computer to put a special character in the middle of the screen. I want the computer to move the character around randomly.

You know that you will see a line for the random number generator. This time we will use numbers between one and four. One will stand for up; two, for down; three, for left; four, for right.

Two other variables used in the program are a variable for the number of lines on your screen and a variable for the number of columns or characters on a line. You will need to change these variables to fit your computer. You will need to change the numbers in lines 60 and 70. We have included remark statements before these two lines to help you make the changes. The variable F$ names the character that is being printed. You can change "X" to any other character you wish to use. The N$ variable prints a blank in the space where the character was just printed to erase the character before printing it at a new spot.

Here is the beginning of the program:

```
10 REM  PROGRAM  MOVEIT
20 LET C$=CHR$ (12)
40 LET H=4
50 LET L=1
55 REM SET THE NUMBER OF LINES ON THE NEXT LINE
60 LET S=30
65 REM SET THE NUMBER OF CHARACTERS ON A LINE BELOW
70 LET C=64
80 LET F$=''X''
90 LET N$=''  ''
```

55

The next part of the program is used to define the special characters used to move the cursor. These lines may change for your computer. We have included the statements used on our computer. You will find the lines needed for several computers in the appendix.

```
100 REM CURSOR CONTROL KEYS DEFINED NEXT
105 REM TO MOVE UP
110 LET U$=CHR$ (23)
115 REM TO MOVE DOWN
120 LET D$=CHR$(26)
125 REM TO MOVE LEFT
130 LET L$=CHR$(1)
135 REM TO MOVE RIGHT
140 LET R$=CHR$(19)
```

The rest of the program moves the character around.

```
150 PRINT C$
160 FOR J=1 TO S/2
170 PRINT
180 NEXT J
190 PRINT TAB (C/2); F$;
200 N=INT((H-L+1)*RND (2))+L
210 PRINT L$;N$;
220 IF N=1 THEN PRINT U$;F$;
230 IF N=2 THEN PRINT D$;F$;
240 IF N=3 THEN PRINT L$;F$;
250 IF N=4 THEN PRINT R$;F$;
260 GOTO 200
270 END
```

When the program is run a strange thing will happen. After the program prints about 250 characters, the cursor will suddenly go down to a new line. This change happens because BASIC will only let you PRINT a line with 255 characters or less. Since all of our PRINT lines end with the ";", they tell BASIC not to go to a new line. After printing about 250 characters, BASIC will automatically go to a new line.

For many computers one does not have to use PRINT to put

56

information on the screen. For many computers the information to be put on the screen is stored in memory. These computers use what is called memory-mapped video. If we know where in memory the information goes, we can put information there ourselves without using the PRINT statement. We need a new statement called the POKE statement. The POKE statement pokes a value into a memory location. For our computer the screen memory starts at location 61568. If we type in the line:

```
POKE 61568,72
```

we will see the character "H" printed at the top left corner of the screen. If your computer has a memory mapped video you can use MOVEIT2.

MOVEIT 2 Program

The MOVEIT2 Program is a lot like MOVEIT. The idea sentence is the same. However, the computer needs some different information. It needs to know where screen memory starts and ends and it needs to have a different description of the character it is going to display. It needs the number value of the character. The values for all characters is usually found by using the ASC function. The ASC function is included in lines 110, 185, 200. The POKE statement is included in these same lines.

```
10 REM   PROGRAM   MOVEIT2
20 REM      MEMORY MAPPED VERSION OF MOVEIT
30 LET C$=CHR$ (12)
40 LET C=64
42 LET H=4
44 LET L=1
50 LET F$=''X''
60 LET N$='' ''
65 REM THE NEXT LINE IS FOR START OF SCREEN RAM
70 LET M1=61568
75 REM THE NEXT LINE IS FOR END OF SCREEN RAM
80 LET M2=63487
90 PRINT C$
```

```
100 LET P=(M1+M2) / 2-C/2
110 POKE P, ASC(F$)
120 LET N=INT ((H+L-1)*RND (1)) +L
130 IF N=1 THEN LET P1=P-C
140 IF N=2 THEN LET P1=P+C
150 IF N=3 THEN LET P1=P-1
160 IF N=4 THEN LET P1=P+1
```

The next lines make sure that the random movement of the cursor does not call for pokes that are outside of the screen memory area.

```
170 IF P1>M2 THEN LET P1=M1
180 IF P1<M1 THEN LET P1=M2
185 POKE P, ASC (N$)
190 LET P=P1
200 POKE P, ASC(F$)
210 GOTO 120
220 END
```

If you removed line 185 you would no longer have the blank to erase your character. All the characters poked to the screen would remain and fill up your screen randomly.

FIGURE Program

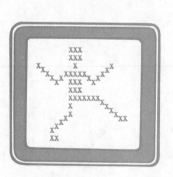

The next program is a program that lets you draw a simple figure to move around the screen. This is a good program to modify using the graphics characters on your computer. We have used subroutines to make modification easy. The program idea for the program is:

I want the computer to let me draw a figure using any characters I choose. I want to be able to move the figure to any place on the screen.

The program needs to do two major tasks. The first task is to draw the picture; the second is to move the figure around. To make it easy for you to change the program, we have placed the lines for these two tasks in subroutines. After the initial setup lines, you will see the main part of the program that sends the computer to the subroutines. Because the program uses an array, the setup part of the program includes lines to define the array. It includes lines to define the clear screen and send-the-cursor-home commands. It also includes lines to tell the computer how large the screen is and where to start drawing the object. You know from the earlier programs that you may need to change some of the numbers on these lines. Here is the first part of the program:

```
10 REM  PROGRAM  FIGURE
20 LET S=4
30 DIM L$ (7,7)
40 LET C$=CHR$(12)
50 LET H$=CHR$(17)
60 LET LM=30
70 LET CM=63
80 LET L=1
90 LET C=0
100 GOSUB 400
110 PRINT C$
120 GOSUB 600
130 GOSUB 800
140 GOTO 120
```

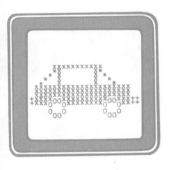

Lines 100 to 140 are really the commands of the program. You can see that most of the commands send the computer to the subroutines. The subroutines do the actual work of the program. The first subroutine reads data statements to put the information into the array that defines the object. The READ statements sends the computer to the DATA statements. The DATA statements include the actual "picture" that you have drawn. We have drawn a simple car using regular typewriter characters. You might want to use your own special graphics to draw a picture that looks a lot more like a real object. Here is what our picture will look like:

```
      _____
     !        !
 _____
     0        0
```

The picture must fit into a grid that is four squares by four squares. You can make the grid larger by changing the varia-

59

ble S on line 20. Line 30, the DIM statement, is set for a maximum size of seven squares by seven squares. You could change the DIM statement to make an even larger figure, but if the figure is too large you may have difficulty moving it around the screen. The subroutine lines follow. The DATA statements are at the end of the program.

```
399 REM SUBROUTINE TO SET UP THE OBJECT
400 FOR J=1 TO S
410 FOR K=1 TO S
420 READ L$ (J,K)
430 NEXT K
440 NEXT J
450 RETURN
```

The next subroutine prints the object on the screen. It is unlikely that you would want to change the lines in this subroutine.

```
599 REM   SUBR TO PRINT THE OBJECT
600 PRINT C$;
610 FOR J=1 TO L
620 PRINT
630 NEXT J
640 FOR J=1 TO S
650 PRINT TAB(C);L$(J,1);
660 FOR K=2 TO S
670 PRINT L$(J,K);
680 NEXT K
690 PRINT
700 NEXT J
710 RETURN
```

The next subroutine lets us tell the computer how to move the object. You will need to use the letters "U," "D," "R," and "L" to tell the computer which way to move.

```
799 REM SUBROUTINE TO GET MOVEMENT OF CURSOR
800 PRINT H$
810 INPUT M$
820 IF M$=''U'' THEN LET L=L-1
```

```
830  IF M$=''L'' THEN LET C=C−1
840  IF M$=''R'' THEN LET C=C+1
850  IF M$=''D'' THEN LET L=L+1
860  IF M$=''L'' OR M$=''R'' OR M$=''U'' THEN GOTO 890
870  IF M$=''D'' THEN GOTO 890
880  GOTO 800
890  IF L<=0 THEN L=LM−2
900  IF L>LM THEN LET L=1
910  IF C<0 THEN LET C=CM−2
920  IF C>CM THEN LET C=0
930  RETURN
```

Line 810 tells the computer to get the letter for the direction you want to move. The letter must be followed by pushing the return key because the INPUT statement always needs the information followed by a return. If you have a special statement to read the keyboard without using a return, you can change the INPUT statement to the new statement. You will find that the picture moves without the INPUT question mark prompt. The special statement may be a GET statement or an INKEY$ function. You will need to have an IF statement on the same line. The changed line might look like one of these two lines:

```
810  GET M$: IFM$='' '' THEN GOTO 810
```

or

```
810  M$=INKEY$: IF M$='' '' THEN GOTO 810
```

The last part of the program includes the DATA statements used to define the picture. You will want to change these lines to draw your own pictures. An easy way to decide how to draw your picture with regular typewriter keys or graphics symbols is to use a paper grid. You need a grid with the same number of squares as the computer expects. A 4×4 grid has four squares across and four squares down. A 7×7 grid has seven squares across and seven squares down. Here is a 4×4 grid and 7×7 grid that you can copy and use to try out your pictures before changing the DATA statements.

61

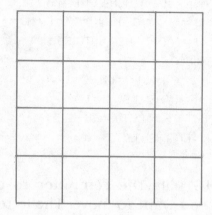

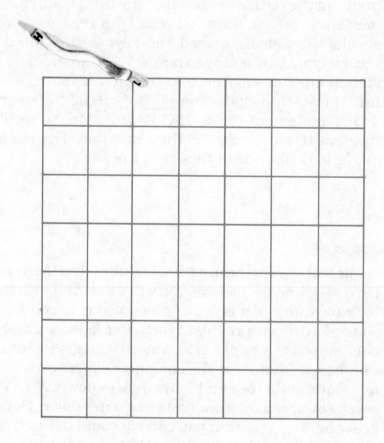

Here are the program lines written to make the simple car.

```
999  REM NEXT DEFINE THE OBJECT WITH DATA STATEMENTS 4X4
1000 DATA "  ","  _","   ","  _","   "
1010 DATA " !"," "," ","  !"
1020 DATA " _","  _","  _","  _"
1030 DATA " 0","  "," "," 0"
2000 END
```

After you have typed in this program you will want to change the picture. You might want to have more than a 4×4 grid. It would be easy to save the program without any DATA statements. Then you could recall the program from your mass storage device and add the data statements to draw the picture you want. You should leave line 999 to remind you to add the data statements. You might want to add a remark line at the beginning of the program, too.

SQUAREIT Program

This last program is a simple game program. The game is simple. The program is not simple. The game is like an old squares game that people play on paper with a pencil. The players draw a game board by putting dots on the paper to stand for the corners of squares. The players then take turns drawing lines between the dots. The player who completes a box or square marks the box as his or hers. The winner of the game is the one who makes the most boxes. Your computer can draw the game board for you, but you cannot draw lines on your computer screen with a pencil. You can tell the computer where you want the lines. You will have to tell the computer which square you want and where to draw the line. In this game, you will tell which square you want by giving the row and the column of the square. You will tell where to draw the line by telling the computer to draw the up, down, left or right line.

The game is simple but the program is complex and it is much longer than all the other programs in this book. It has several subroutines that are at the beginning of the program rather than at the end. The subroutines come first so that the program can run faster. When a program is short, you can

63

put the subroutines at the end of the program or at the beginning. Where you put the subroutines does not make a difference in how long the computer takes to read in the subroutine. But when a program is long, the computer takes more time to find the subroutines if they are at the end of the program. Why? Because when it is told to look for a subroutine, the computer begins at the first line of the program and reads all the lines until it finds the line for the subroutine. The computer will have to read fewer lines if the subroutines are at the beginning of the program.

The program idea for SQUAREIT is:

I want the computer to let a friend and I play a game in which we each have a chance to complete squares. The game will be played on a game board of dots that represent squares that could be completed. We will alternate turns at drawing one of the four lines that make a square. The person who draws the line to complete a square will win that square. I want the computer to mark each completed square to show who won it. The computer will need to check each line drawn to be sure it can be drawn. It should also count the squares that each player has at the end of the game.

This program uses four new BASIC functions. The first function is similar to LEFT$. It is the MID$ function. While the LEFT$ function told the computer to look at characters in a string beginning at the left of the string, MID$ tells the computer to look at characters in the middle of the string. You must tell the computer what you mean by "middle." You tell the computer to start looking at a particular character in the string. The computer calls the first character one and counts to whatever character you say is the start of the "middle." You must also tell the computer where the "middle" ends. You tell it that the "middle" ends after it counts the number of characters you tell it to. You might tell the computer that the "middle" begins at three and includes four characters or that it begins at six and includes three characters. MID$ and LEFT$ are the same functions if you tell the computer that the "middle" begins at character one.

Just as when you used LEFT$, you must tell the computer the string that it must use with MID$. There is also a RIGHT$ function. It is not included in this program but you can guess that it is like LEFT$ function except that the computer looks at the right end of the string. A MID$ line looks like this:

```
123 LET A$=''ABCDEFG''
124 LET B$=MID$(A$,3,2)
125 PRINT B$
```

Do you know what will be printed by line 125? The middle of the string called A$ will be printed. The A$ string is "ABCDEFG." But what is the "middle?" The "middle" begins at the third character and is two characters long. That means that B$ is the string "CD." Your computer would print "CD." If you change the "3" and the "2" in the MID$ expression you can print different letters. If you write line 124 as

```
124 LET B$=MID$(A$,2,3)
```

you would print "BCD."

The second function is LEN. Notice that this fuction does not have a dollar sign. It is going to give you a number, not a string or list of characters. The number it will give you is the length of a string. The computer will count the number of characters in the string you ask it to look at. You tell it what string to count by putting the string name in parenthesis after the function like this:

```
126 LET X=LEN(A$)
127 PRINT X
```

If you include these lines with the lines above, the computer will tell you that A$ is 7 characters long.

The last two functions are used with PRINT. They are TAB and SPC. TAB tells the computer to move over to the column number to which you tell it to move. You tell the computer where to move by putting the column number in parenthesis after TAB. Most computers have the TAB function. Some computers also have the SPC function. SPC stands for space and tells the computer to put in as many spaces as you have indicated in parenthesis after SPC. If your computer does not have an SPC function, you can use the LEFT$ function to include the number of spaces you need. You define the variable SP$ as a lot of spaces and then use the LEFT$ function to include the number of spaces you need. Instead of one line you will need two but if you use the SPC function more than once, you will only need one variable line. You could include the string of spaces at the beginning of the program in the setup section. Here is how the line would look:

```
15 LET SP$='                 '
```

Your line to replace the program line with the SPC function that looks like this:

```
128 PRINT SPC(7); ''HELLO''
```

would look like this:

```
128 PRINT LEFT$(SP$,7); ''HELLO''
```

The program begins with a setup section that names and gives dimensions to the important variables used in the program. The first variable is NS. NS stands for number of squares to be used in the game. NS=3 means that the game will be played with three rows and three columns. B$ is an array that has the picture of the game board. C$ and H$ are variables you have seen before. They are the clear screen and home the cursor variables. You may need to set them for your computer. TA is a variable to tell where to start the game board. Line 30 tells the computer to reserve extra space in memory for the string variables that will be used in this program. We never needed to worry about the amount of string space in our other programs because we always had short strings. Line 90 tells the computer to find line 10000 to find the main part of the program. The computer will skip over all the lines before line 10000. These lines that are skipped are the lines for the subroutines which the computer will find when the main part of the program uses one of them. Here is the setup part of the program:

```
10 REM  SQUARE-IT
```

```
20  REM SET LINE 40   WITH SIZE OF BOARD
30  CLEAR(300)
40  LET NS=3
50  DIM B$(NS*2+3)
60  LET C$=CHR$(12)
70  LET H$=CHR$(17)
80  TA=10
90  GOTO 10000
```

The next part of the program is a subroutine to write the game board on the screen. Every time your friend or you make a move, the board must be rewritten on the screen to show the change. This subroutine is the one most frequently used and so it comes first.

```
4000  REM SUBROUTINE TO RE-WRITE BOARD TO SCREEN
4010  PRINT C$
4020  FOR J=1 TO NS*2+1+2
4030  PRINT TAB (TA);B$(J)
4040  NEXT J
4050  RETURN
```

The next two subroutines print messages when you make a mistake while playing the game.

```
4500  REM SUBROUTINE WRONG SQUARE LOCATION ERROR MESSAGE
4510  PRINT H$
4520  FOR J=1 TO NS*2+4: PRINT: NEXT J
4530  IF R>NS THEN PRINT ''ROW TOO LARGE'';
4540  IF C>NS THEN PRINT ''COLUMN TOO LARGE'';
4545  IF C<=0 OR R<=0 THEN PRINT ''1 OR BIGGER..'';
4550  PRINT SPC(25)
4560  FOR J=1 TO 500
4570  NEXT J
4580  RETURN
4600  REM SUBROUTINE   WRONG LINE ERROR MESSAGE
4610  PRINT H$
4620  FOR J=1 TO NS*2+4: PRINT: NEXT J
4630  PRINT ''INCORRECT ENTRY-TRY AGAIN
4640  FOR J=1 TO 500
```

```
4650 NEXT J
4660 RETURN
```

The next three subroutines are used to find out what move a player wants to make.

```
5000 REM SUBROUTINE SEE IF SELECTED LINE ALREADY MARKED
5010 LET E=1
5020 LET Z2=2*R+2
5030 LET Z3=2*C
5040 IF D$=''U'' AND MID$(B$(Z2-1),Z3,1)='' ''THEN LET
     E=0
5050 IF D$=''D'' AND MID$(B$(Z2+1),Z3,1)='' ''THEN LET
     E=0
5060 IF D$=''L'' AND MID$(B$(Z2),Z3-1,1)='' ''THEN LET
     E=0
5070 IF D$=''R'' AND MID$(B$(Z2),Z3+1,1)='' ''THEN LET
     E=0
5080 RETURN
5200 REM SUBROUTINE TO FIND OUT WHICH SQUARE WANTED
5210 LET E=0
5220 PRINT H$
5230 FOR J=1 TO NS*2+4: PRINT : NEXT J
5240 PRINT ''ROW AND COLUMN OF SQUARE''; SPC(6);
5250 FOR J=1 TO 6: PRINT CHR$(8);: NEXT J
5260 INPUT R,C
5270 IF R>NS OR C>NS THEN LET E=1
5280 IF R<=NS AND C<=NS THEN LET E=0
5285 IF R<=0 OR C<=0 THEN LET E=1
5290 IF E=1 THEN GOSUB 4500
5300 IF  R, U, D ''; SPC(6);
5310 RETURN
5400 REM SUBROUTINE LOCATION IN THE SQUARE TO MARK
5410 PRINT H$
5420 FOR J=1 TO NS*2+4: PRINT : NEXT J
5430 PRINT ''MARK L,R,U,D''; SPC(6);
5440 FOR J=1 TO 6: PRINT CHR$ (8);: NEXT J
5450 INPUT D$
5460 IF D$=''L'' OR D$=''R'' THEN GOTO 5490
```

I WON!

```
5465  IF D$=''U'' OR D$=''D'' THEN GOTO 5490
5470  GOSUB 4600
5480  GOTO 5410
5490  RETURN
```

The next six subroutines put the line that has been chosen into the array, and check to see if a square or squares are finished by adding the line. If a square or squares are finished, the program marks them with the number of the winner and adds a counter to the total score of the player. There are also two error message routines included in the six.

```
5600  REM   MARK THE ENTRY IN THE BOARD ARRAY
5610  IF D$=''U'' THEN
      LET B$(2*R+1)=LEFT$(B$(2*R+1),2*C-1) + ''-'' +
        MID$(B$(2*R+1),2*C+1,2*NS+6)
5620  IF D$=''D'' THEN
      LET B$(2*R+3)=LEFT$(B$(2*R+3),2*C-1) + ''-'' +
        MID$(B$(2*R+3),2*C+1,2*NS+6)
5630  IF D$=''L'' THEN
      LET B$(2*R+2)=LEFT$(B$(2*R+2),2*C-2) + ''!'' +
        MID$(B$(2*R+2),2*C,2*NS+6)
5640  IF D$=''R'' THEN
      LET B$(2*R+2)=LEFT$(B$(2*R+2),2*C) + ''!'' +
        MID$(B$(2*R+2),2*C+2,2*NS+6)
5650  RETURN
5700  REM SUBROUTINE SEE IF SQUARE IS FINISHED
5710  LET M1=1
5720  IF MID$(B$(2*R+1),2*C,1)='' ''
        OR MID$(B$(2*R+3),2*C,1)='' ''
      THEN LET M1=0
5730  IF MID$(B$(2*R+2),2*C-1,1)='' ''
        OR MID$(B$(2*R+2),2*C+1,1)='' ''
      THEN LET M1=0
5740  RETURN
5900  REM SQUARE DONE-MARK CENTER, ADD 1 TO SCORE
5910  LET B$(2*R+2)=LEFT$(B$(2*R+2),2*C-1)+
        CHR$(PL+48)+MID$(B$,2*R+2),2*C+1,2*NS+6)
```

69

```
5920 IF PL=1 THEN LET S1=S1+1
5930 IF PL=2 THEN LET S2=S2+1
5940 RETURN
6000 REM   PLACE ALREADY MARKED ERROR MESSAGE
6010 PRINT H$
6020 FOR J=1 TO NS*2+4: PRINT : NEXT J
6030 PRINT ''THAT LOCATION ALREADY USED    ''
6040 FOR J=1 TO 500
6050 NEXT J
6060 RETURN
6500 REM   SQUARE ALREADY FILLED ERROR MESSAGE
6510 PRINT H$
6520 FOR J=1 TO NS*2+4: PRINT : NEXT J
6530 PRINT ''THAT SQUARE COMPLETED !!''; SPC(10)
6540 FOR J=1 TO 500
6550 NEXT J
6560 RETURN
7000 REM   SEE IF CURRENT OR ADJACENT SQUARE IS FINISHED
7010 GOSUB 5700
7020 IF M1=1 THEN GOSUB 5OSUB 5900
7055 IF M1=1 THEN LET M1=0
7060 LET C=C+2
7070 IF S$=''R'' AND C< >(NS+1) THEN GOSUB 5700
7080 IF M1=1 THEN GOSUB 5900
7085 IF M1=1 THEN LET M1=0
7090 LET C=C—1: LET R=R—1
7100 IF D$=''U'' AND R< >0 THEN GOSUB 5700
7100 IF M1=1 THEN GOSUB 5900
7115 IF M1=1 THE LET M1=0
7120 LET R=R+2
7130 IF D$=''D'' AND R< >(NS+1) THEN GOSUB 5700
7140 IF M1=1 THEN GOSUB 5900
7145 IF M1=1 THEN LET M1=0
7150 LET R=R—1
7160 RETURN
```

The next subroutine asks for the names of the players. When you play the game, the computer marks the squares you complete with either a one or a two. When it tells you that it is your turn, it gives both your number and your name.

```
9100  REM GET NAMES OF PLAYERS
9100  FOR J=1 TO 10: PRINT :NEXT J
9140  INPUT ''NAME OF PLAYER 1'';X$
9150  LET X$=X$+''         ''
9170  INPUT ''NAME OF PLAYER 2'';Y$
9180  LET Y$=Y$+''         ''
9190  FOR J=1 TO 500
9200  NEXT J
9210  PRINT C$
9220  RETURN
```

The final subroutine builds the complete board for the game from DATA statements at the very end of the program. The first part of the subroutine reads in a 3×3 game board from the DATA statements. If you use more than a 3×3 board, the next part of the routine builds the part of the board greater than 3×3. The last lines of the routine print the name of the game and set the score counters, S1 and S2, to zero.

```
9500  REM SUBROUTINE TO SET UP THE GAME BOARD
9510  PRINT C$
9520  IF NS<3 THEN LET NS=3
9530  FOR J=1 TO 9
9540  READ B$(J)
9550  NEXT J
9560  IF NS=3 IF THEN GOTO 9680
9570  REM NEXT LINES CAN INCREASE BOARD SIZE
9580  FOR J=10 TO NS*2+3
9590  LET B$(J)=B$(J-2)
9600  NEXT J
9610  LET P$=''              '': LET P$=LEFT$(P$,(NS-3)*2+1)
9620  LET Q$=B$(9)+B$(9)
9630  LET Q$=LEFT$(Q$,(NS-3)*2)
9632  LET R$=''4 5 6 7 8 ''
9634  LET L1=1
9640  FOR J=3 TO NS*2+2 STEP 2
9650  LET B$(J)=LEFT$(B$(J),8)+Q$
9660  LET B$(J+1)=LEFT$(B$(J+1),7)+P$+STR$(L1)
```

```
9665 LET L1=L1+1
9670 NEXT J
9672 LET B$(NS*2+3)=LEFT$(B$(NS*2+3),8)+Q$
9674 LET B$(5)=LEFT$(B$(5),NS*2+1) + ''    ROW''
9676 LET B$(2)=B$(2)+LEFT$(R$,(NS-3)*2)
9680 REM    NEED THIS FOR A GOTO STATEMENT
9685 REM NEXT LINES GIVE THE GAME TITLE AND SET COUNTERS
9690 FOR J=1 TO 5: PRINT :NEXT J
9700 PRINT TAB(10); ''SQUARE-IT''
9710 FOR J=1 TO 5 :PRINT :NEXT J
9720 PRINT ''C 1982 BY D&P HARRIS''
9730 FOR J=1 TO 500
9740 NEXT J
9750 PRINT C$
9760 LET S1=0
9770 LET S2=0
9780 RETURN
```

Now that you have seen all the subroutines, you are ready to see the main part of the program. You can guess that this part will have a lot of GOSUB Lines. Can you guess how many GOSUB Lines? There are fewer GOSUB lines that subroutines. There are thirteen GOSUB lines and GOSUB 4000 is used twice. All the subroutines are included once on a GOSUB line. But there are fourteen subroutines, two more than used in the main part of the program. Do you know where the other subroutines are used? They are used in other subroutines. This is a complex program. It has many subroutines and some of the subroutines use other subroutines.

```
10000 REM ***********************************
10010 REM THE MAIN PART OF THE PROGRAM
10020 GOSUB 9500
10030 GOSUB 9100
10040 GOSUB 4000
10050 LET PL=1
10060 REM THE NEXT LINE LETS PLAYER 1 GO FIRST
10070 LET Z$=X$
```

```
10080  REM NEXT LINE CALCULATES THE MOVES IN THE GAME
10090  LET NM=2*NS*(NS+1)
10100  REM START OF FOR-NEXT LOOP FOR THE ACTUAL GAME
10110  FOR I=1 TO NM
10120  PRINT H$;
10125  FOR J=1 TO 2*NS+4: PRINT :NEXT J
10130  PRINT ''PLAYER '';PL;''   '';Z$
10140  GOSUB 5200
10150  GOSUB 5700
10160  IF M1=0 THEN GOTO 10190
10170  GOSUB 6500
10180  GOTO 10140
10190  GOSUB 5400
10200  GOSUB 5000
10210  IF E=0 THEN GOTO 10240
10220  GOSUB 6000
10230  GOTO 10190
10240  GOSUB 5600
10250  GOSUB 7000
10260  IF M1=0 THEN GOTO 10280
10270  GOSUB 5900
10280  GOSUB 4000
10290  IF PL=1 THEN LET Z$=Y$
10300  IF PL=2 THEN LET Z$=X$
10310  IF PL=1 THEN LET PL=2 : GOTO 10330
10320  LET PL=1
10330  NEXT I
10340  REM   GAME OVER   GIVE FINAL MESSAGE
10350  PRINT H$
10360  FOR J=1 TO NS*2+4: PRINT :NEXT J
10370  PRINT ''PLAYER 1 HAD   '';S1;'' SQUARES FINISHED''
10380  PRINT ''PLAYER 2 HAD   '';S2;'' SQUARES FINISHED''
10390  PRINT: PRINT ''TYPE   RUN   TO PLAY AGAIN''
10400  GOTO 20090
10410  REM END OF THE GAME   ***********
10420  REM NEXT ARE DATA STATEMENTS FOR 3X3 BOARD
20000  DATA ''COLUMN''
20010  DATA ''  1  2  3  ''
```

```
20020 DATA ".....  "
20030 DATA "     1 "
20040 DATA ".....  ROW"
20050 DATA "     2 "
20060 DATA ".....  "
20070 DATA "     3 "
20080 DATA ".....  "
20090 END
```

When you type in this long program you will want to be sure to check the notes in the Appendix to see if there are any specific changes that must be made for your computer. Some computers need to use PRINT AT statements to replace the statements for home and tab. Some computers have special requirements when you want to work with strings. Check the Appendix for information on six popular computers; the Apple II+, the VIC Color Computer, the Timex Sinclair 1000, the Texas Instruments Computer, the Radio Shack Computers and the Atari Computers. You will find a chart summarizing the BASIC statements and functions and giving some other information. Also, notes are included on some of the changes that need to be made in the program for these computers. Have fun using the ideas in this chapter to write your own programs.

HAPPY COMPUTING!

Appendix

Basic Statements and Functions for Six Computers

STATEMENTS	APPLE II+	VIC COLOR	TIMEX	TEXAS INSTR.	ATARI	RADIO SHACK
PRINT	same	same	same	same	same	same
INPUT	same	same	same	same	same	same
READ	same	same	NO	same	special	same
DATA	same	same	NO	same	same	same
LET	opt.	opt.	needed	opt.	opt.	opt.
DIM	same	same	special	same	special	same
FOR	same	same	same	same	same	same
NEXT	same	same	same	same	same	same
STOP	same	same	same	same	same	same
END	same	same	NO	same	same	same
REM	same	same	same	same	same	same
GOTO	same	same	same	same	same	same
GOSUB	same	same	same	same	same	same
RETURN	same	same	same	same	same	same
POKE	same	same	same	same	same	same
IF...THEN	same	same	IF key THEN key	same special	same	same

FUNCTIONS	APPLE II+	VIC COLOR	TIMEX	TEXAS INSTR.	ATARI	RADIO SHACK
LEFT$	same	same	special	special	special	same
RIGHT$	same	same	special	special	special	same
MID$	same	same	special	special	special	same
CHR$	same	same	same	same	same	same
ASC	same	same	CODE KEY	same	same	same
LEN	same	same	same	same	same	same
TAB	same	same	same	same	no	same
SPC	same	same	no	no	no	no
INT	same	same	same	same	same	same
RND	same	same	same	special	special	same

OTHER	APPLE II+	VIC COLOR	TIMEX	TEXAS INSTR.	ATARI	RADIO SHACK
HOME	VTABI command	CHR$(19)	PRINT AT 0,0	use calls	POSITION 0,0	PRINT@ 0
CLEAR SCREEN	HOME command	CHR$(147)	CHR$(251)	use calls	GR.0	CLS
SCREEN MEMORY START	NOT EASILY	7680	NOT MEMORY MAPPED	NOT MEMORY MAPPED	NOT EASILY	15360+0 (III)
SCREEN MEMORY END	NOT EASILY	8185	NOT MEMORY MAPPED	NOT MEMORY MAPPED	NOT EASILY	15360 +1023 (III)
CURSOR LEFT	use HTAB command	CHR$(157)	use PRINT AT	NOT EASY	CHR$ (30)	use PRINT@
CURSOR RIGHT	use HTAB command	CHR$(29)	use PRINT AT	NOT EASY	CHR$ (31)	use PRINT@
CURSOR UP	use VTAB command	CHR$(145)	use PRINT AT	NOT EASY	CHR$ (28)	use PRINT@
CURSOR DOWN	use VTAB command	CHR$(17)	use PRINT AT	NOT EASY	CHR$ (29)	use PRINT@
RUN	same	RUN STOP KEY	same	same	same	same
STOP A PROGRAM	CONTROL C	RUN STOP KEY	BREAK OR STOP	FUNCTION 4	BREAK	BREAK
SINGLE CHARACTER INPUT	GET	GET	INKEY$	no	no	INKEY$

Other Information on the Computers and Programs

APPLE II

The programs generally run on the APPLE II with very few changes. The most important change is that you must use the special commands to home the cursor and clear the screen (see the table). The PRINT CHR$(xxx) are not used to move the cursor. HTAB and VTAB are used instead. Whenever a program has these commands you should substitute the correct Apple command.

VIC COLOR COMPUTER

The programs should run on the VIC just as they are written. Just remember to change the CHR$ values to those in the tables above.

TIMEX

You must use the LET statement with the Timex computer. You must also tell the computer what each variable is equal to. To use the variable A, you must include the statement LET A=0. The TIMEX can have only one variable for a DIM statement so when programs say: DIM A(2), B(4) you must write the information on two lines using two DIM statements. With a string array you must tell the computer how long your strings will be. You must add an extra number to the DIM statement. In the program the DIM statement would look like this: DIM A$(2). In your program the statement would look like this: DIM A$(2,20). The 20 would tell the computer that the longest string is not more than 20 characters long. The Timex computer uses the form A$(N1 to N2) to accomplish the same functions as the three separate functions listed as RIGHT$, LEFT$ and MID$. Remember that the TIMEX keys are labeled with the command words. They do not have to be typed in. To use the random number program use the RND command without a number in parentheses.

TEXAS INSTRUMENTS

The TEXAS INSTRUMENTS computer can have only one statement per line. If you find a program line with two statements, just divide the statements into two lines. The IF …THEN lines in all programs must also be changed. The programs are written with statements following the THEN statement like this:

```
120 IF A$=''NO'' THEN PRINT ''CORRECT''.
```

You must change the line to remove the PRINT statement. Your line would look like this:

```
120 IF A$-''NO'' THEN 121 ELSE 130
121 PRINT ''CORRECT''
```

Line 130 would be the next line of the program after line 120 and would not have to change unless, of course, it also was an IF…THEN line.

The TEXAS INSTRUMENTS computer also uses the SEG$ command to take the place of RIGHT$, LEFT$ and MID$. The command is written SEGA (N1,N2) which tells the computer to take a part of the string called A$. In place of N1, put the number of the character of the string that you want the computer to take first. N2 should be replaced by the number of the character where you want the computer to stop.

ATARI

For the ATARI computers, all string variables must be initialized so you must use a DIM statement for all of the string variables in a program. The DIM statement should be used to tell the computer the maximum number of characters in any string.

The ATARI also uses the one command to take the place of RIGHT$, LEFT$ and MID$. The command is written without a special command word and looks like this: A$(N1,N2). This line tells the computer to take a part of the string called A$. In place of N1 you should put the number of the character of the string that you want the computer to take first. N2 should be replaced by the number of the character where you want the computer to stop. You can put any command in front of the string variable. You could use the command PRINT A$(N1,N2).

When you want to use the random number generator, you must first use RANDOMIZE and then use RND with no number in parentheses after the command.

RADIO SHACK

To use the programs on the RADIO SHACK computers, you need to make only a few changes. To send the cursor to home, you must use PRINT@ 0 in place of CHR$(xx). To move the cursor around, you use PRINT@ followed by the space where you want the cursor to move. To clear the screen, you use CLS instead of CHR$(xx).

INKEY$ replaces GET in all programs.

INDEX